Little Brown Girl
by Behnush Mortimer, Ph.D.

Write Away Books, Carlsbad, CA

Copyright © 2025 by Behnush Mortimer.

All rights reserved. No part of this publication may be reproduced or transmitted in any form or by any means, electronic or mechanical, including photocopying, recording, or by any information storage and retrieval system, without prior written permission from the publisher.

This book is available at quantity discounts for bulk purchases of promotional applications. For information, contact rob@writeawaybooks.com.

Published by Write Away Books, USA

www.writeawaybooks.com
PO Box 1681, Carlsbad, CA 92018

Print ISBN: 979-8-9896431-4-1
First Edition

Book and Cover Design by Gritton Design

Dedicated to
my little girl Cara and to
our rock and protector,
my husband Damon

Little Brown Girl
by Behnush Mortimer, Ph.D.

When I was one I had big brown eyes that everyone adored. I saw smiles all around me and clouds up above.

I felt so loved and could not wait to see more of the world. And when I saw the moon, my mom would kiss me goodnight.

When I was three my little brown legs loved to run. I was eager to explore and went all around the yard chasing butterflies. I enjoyed going to the beach with my brother and sister and playing in the sand.

And when I finally got tired, my dad would wrap me in a blanket and rock me to sleep. I felt warm and safe.

When I was six I hugged my dog, waved goodbye to my mom and dad, and went off to my first day of school. I met many new friends and a teacher who said my name funny.

My name is Anoush - pronounced Ah-noosh - but somehow it came out Ah-nows or Ah-nuss.

Argh, NO! I told the teacher the correct way to say my name, but I guess she never heard me. She NEVER got it right!

When I was eight the kids at school started making fun of me. They said my lunch looked and smelled strange. But it was my favorite; beef kabob and roasted tomatoes. And even though I offered, nobody would even try a bite.

Sometimes I'd get sad, realizing our Persian culture made my family stand apart from other people. Was it the food, the music, and our language...or was it just because I felt so different from everyone else?

Of course, I didn't really care who or what you were. I played with a special group of friends who were each unique in their own way. We were all made up of different colors and cultures.

But none of that was important to any of us, because everyone was nice and we made each other laugh.

When I was 10 my family moved to a new town. I was not too excited for the change because I was leaving my friends behind. All the kids on our new street had yellow hair and light skin. I looked like a chocolate lollipop with my brown skin and dark hair.

GROAN! Now I had to make a WHOLE new bunch of friends, and start all over again. And, while I felt lonely at first, joining the school's soccer team helped me finally feel like I was startng to fit in.

When I was 13 I scored the winning goal in the championship game. All of a sudden I was the hero, and EVERYONE wanted to know me.

After the game, the coach took us all out for pizza and we talked late into the night. Everyone on the team told me what a great job I had done.

Suddenly I was cool, but some of the other kids still made fun of my name and the food I'd bring for lunch. But because I was gettng comfortable with who I was, I no longer cared what they said. I now knew who my real friends were.

When I was 16, my parents threw a big birthday party for me. Everyone I knew was there. All the girls wore pretty dresses and the boys wore jackets and we all danced to every kind of music.

The kids from school saw the fancy desserts and gold rimmed plates, and most of them at least tried some of the Persian food my mother had made. "YUMMY!" they said, and realized what they had been missing. I got lots of happy birthday hugs and felt prouder of my culture and my family than I had ever been before.

Today I am a successful professional; a strong and confident woman with a daughter of my own. And I'm teaching her that even when people make fun of you, or don't understand what you say, or think you're strange merely because you are not like them, their opinions don't matter. What is important is the support of real friends and family and a belief in yourself.

I know now that all of these experiences, from standing up for how my name is pronounced to defending my delicious - and sometimes funny smelling - food, have made me stronger.

Yes, I've felt different and sad at times, but these experiences helped make me who I am today; tough, smart, and secure in who I am.

I am a proud brown girl.

Originally of Persian extraction, Behnush Mortimer knows what it's like to be the one kid who gets made fun of or who nobody understands. Today, as a successful Vocational Rehabilitational Consultant, she is passionate about helping individuals achieve their fullest potential and ensuring they're empowered to reach all their personal and professional life choices.

Behnush lives in Carlsbad CA with her husband, daughter and two dogs. They enjoy spending their time in the sun and at the sea. The best way to find her is at www.rehabsource.org.

"I hope you enjoy reading this as much as I enjoyed writing it."

Behnush Mortimer

www.ingramcontent.com/pod-product-compliance
Lightning Source LLC
Chambersburg PA
CBHW042357030426
42337CB00029B/5127